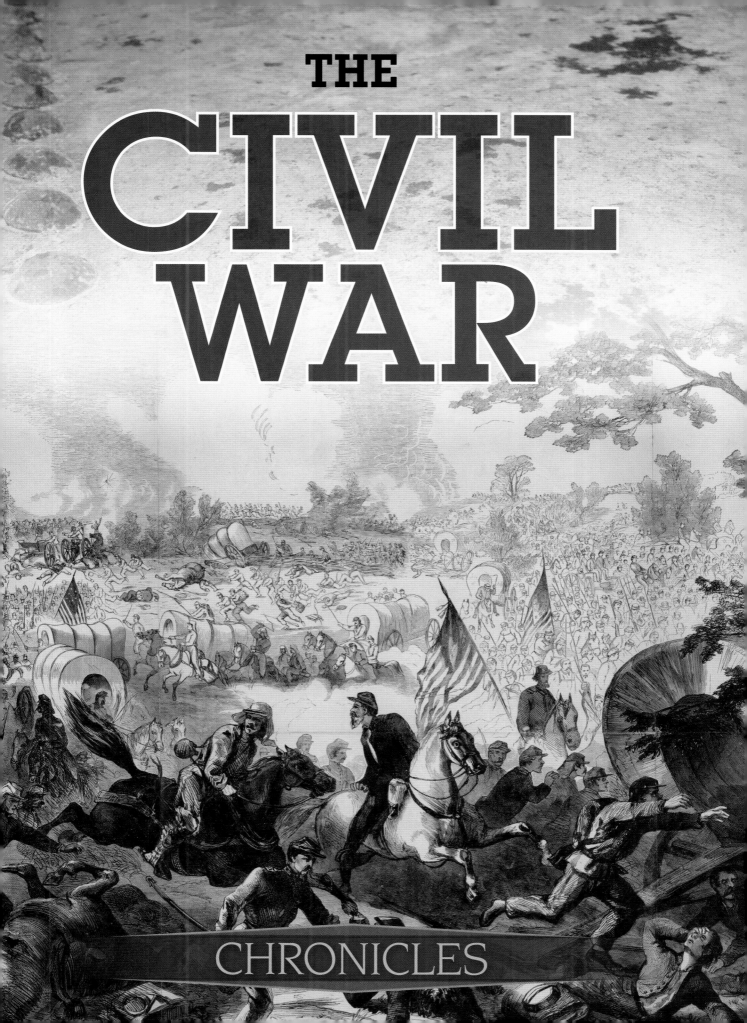

THE CIVIL WAR

CHRONICLES

Contents

2

3

Published by World Publications Group, Inc.
140 Laurel Street
East Bridgewater, MA 02333
www.wrldpub.com

© Instinctive Product Development 2013

Packaged by Instinctive Product Development for World Publications Group, Inc.

Printed in China

ISBN: 978-1-4643-0297-8

Designed by: BrainWave

Creative Director: Kevin Gardner

Written by: Rob Morris and Paul Marcello

Images courtesy of Mary Evans Picture Library and The American Library of Congress

www.maryevans.com

Chapter One:
The Inevitable

There is something very American about the Civil War, something that continues to grab and hold our fascination a century and a half later. It has given us some of our greatest heroes—men like Abraham Lincoln, Robert E. Lee, Ulysses S. Grant, and Stonewall Jackson. Its battles have become part of our lexicon—Bull Run, Shiloh, Gettysburg. Tales of heroism have become part of our national lore. Who has not thrilled at the gallantry of Pickett's Charge or the brave stand of the Union troops at Shiloh's Hornets' Nest? Perhaps part of the fascination lies in the fact that it was Americans against other Americans, or because of its terrible lethality.

The Civil War's death toll continues to surpass that of all America's wars combined. Often called the first modern war, it was fought with Napoleonic tactics that proved no match for the modern weapons of the Industrial Age— weapons that could kill or maim a man a hundred ways. It was a war often fought on the march in forests

■ **ABOVE: The ruins of Gallego Flour Mills, Richmond, VA, April 1865.**

and fields, insect-ridden swamps, and bone-chilling rain. Disease was the war's number one killer. It was a war fought for idealistic American goals like freedom, states' rights, and unity—a war that aroused the best intentions in men but occasionally descended into outright butchery. When the cannon smoke cleared and the din of battle stilled, to be replaced by the call of birds and the rustling of leaves, more than 620,000 Americans lay silent. A third were killed in action, the rest died of disease and other causes. Another 400,000 were wounded. One historian estimates that 10% of all Northern men between 20 and 45 were killed, and 30% of Southern men between 18 and 40. In a nation with a total wartime population of only 31,443,321 in 1860, the number of men who served—and died—meant that hardly a family in the North or South was not intimately and sadly acquainted with war's tragic consequences. If the war's casualties were adjusted to today's population, the US would lose 7 million men. It

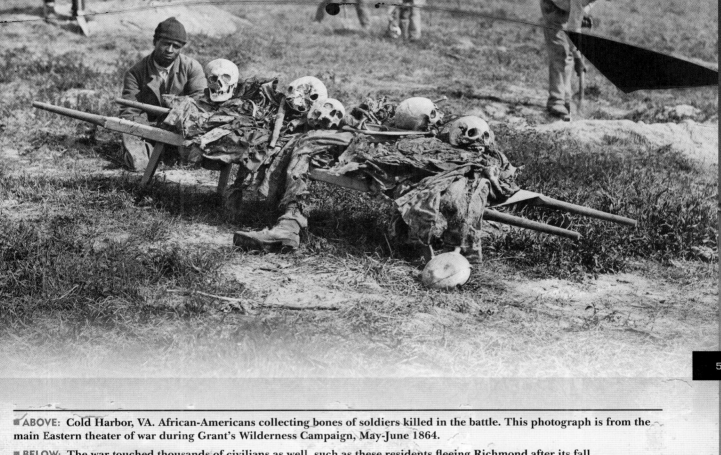

■ ABOVE: Cold Harbor, VA. African-Americans collecting bones of soldiers killed in the battle. This photograph is from the main Eastern theater of war during Grant's Wilderness Campaign, May-June 1864.

■ BELOW: The war touched thousands of civilians as well, such as these residents fleeing Richmond after its fall April 2, 1865.

An account Sales of Fifteen African Slaves
Sold on the 19th of April 1825

No	Name of Slaves	Name Purchasers	Price
1	Peter	Phillip McCostry	661
2	Isaac	Danl S Walden	555
3	Bob	do	600
4	Tom	do	510
5	Billy	do	510
6	Light	do	470
7	Jambosa		495
8	Banjo	Allen Glover	625
9	Friday	William Crawford	510
10	Dick Sale	Danl S Walden	570
11	Joe	do	605
12	William	P Austill	612
13	Perry	Allen Glover	620
14	Dick Boy	do	615
15	Jack Old	P Austill	262
			$8223.00

F. W. Armstrong
M A D

■ ABOVE: An image
showing slave quarters
in 1862.

■ LEFT: A copy of a
slave receipt.

was truly horrible.

Did such a horrible war have to happen? Could it have been avoided, through a combination of foresight and diplomacy? While the question remains open for debate, most historians feel that the war was as inevitable to the young nation as the pains of labor to a new mother or those of a young child becoming an adult.

Americans had tried to avoid this war for decades, managing instead only to delay its coming. In so doing, these well-intentioned delaying efforts may well have increased the carnage. When the American Civil War finally broke out, it did so with an intense fury that no one had imagined, and lasted longer than anyone could have predicted. Men who had previously been brothers and countrymen now killed and maimed each other using all the marvelous new devices of the Industrial Age.

The conflagration smoldered for years as a spark in the dry tinder of the new nation, its small but persistent flame fed by a contradiction: the new nation was committed to the principles of freedom and personal liberty but enslaved a portion of its inhabitants. Adding to this contradiction was the diverging social and economic development of North and South. Originally founded on a common agrarian principal, the sections began drifting apart as the North became more urbanized and industrial. In the North, the distance between farms and cities full of factories seemed to shrink as the region became connected by canals, railroads, and telegraph cables. New waves of immigrants flowed into Northern cities, providing the cheap labor needed to stoke the furnaces of progress. Not so in the South, which remained primarily agricultural, and lagged in transportation and industry. The one great industrial development,

■ **ABOVE:** The city of New York. This print shows many boats on the East River with the view of New York City in the background, c. March 15, 1861.

■ **BELOW:** A large crowd of Irish emigrants gather at the harbor at Queenstown ready to depart for a new life in America, 1874.

ILLUSTRATED
NEWSPAPER

Entered according to Act of Congress, in the year 1857, by Frank Leslie, in the Clerk's Office of the District Court for the Southern District of New York. (Copyrighted, June 25, 1857.)

[PRICE 6 CENTS.

[No. 32.—VOL. IV.]

NEW YORK, SATURDAY, JUNE 27, 1857.

CORRESPONDENTS AND TRAVELLERS

VISIT TO DRED SCOTT—HIS FAMILY—INCIDENTS OF HIS LIFE—DECISION OF THE SUPREME COURT.

MEIZA AND LIZZIE, CHILDREN OF DRED SCOTT.

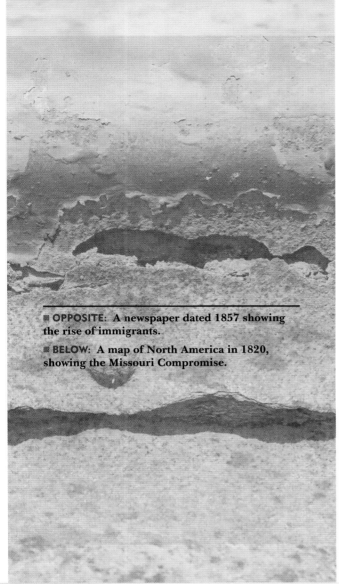

■ **OPPOSITE:** A newspaper dated 1857 showing the rise of immigrants.

■ **BELOW:** A map of North America in 1820, showing the Missouri Compromise.

Eli Whitney's ingenious cotton gin, allowed a single slave to clean 50 pounds of cotton a day rather than one, and opened up the region to King Cotton.

It seemed at times as if where before only one nation had existed, there were now two distinctly separate societies, separated along cultural, economic lines.

In the 1760s, when two surveyors named Charles Mason and Jeremiah Dixon drew their famous Mason-Dixon Line to settle a border dispute between Virginia and Maryland, they unknowingly established an unofficial boundary between North and South. America grew in size and population, the contradictions becoming harder and harder to ignore. Initially, many Northerners disliked slavery and would never consider owning a slave, but were willing to accept its de facto existence in the South. Southern historians correctly point out that the North also used slaves in the 17th and 18th centuries, and that the reason that the North never became

SLAVERY AFTER THE MISSOURI COMPROMISE

- States entirely Free
- States undergoing Gradual Emancipation
- Area Free by Ordinance of 1787
- Area Free by Missouri Compromise
- Slave Area

Dates indicate when freedom was granted, or when gradual abolition began.

And the said husband being now present, aiding and authorising his said wife in the execution of these presents, she the said wife did again declare that she did and doth hereby make a formal renunciation and relinquishment of all her said matrimonial dotal, paraphernal and other rights, claims and privileges in favor of the said *Michael* binding herself and her heirs, at all times, to sustain and acknowledge the validity of this renunciation.

Thus Done and Passed, in my Office, at the city of New Orleans, in the presence of Robt R Daniell and M H Barremore Witnesses of lawful age and domiciliated in this city, who hereunto sign their names with the parties, and me, the said Notary. *This word "not mentioned" on first page, approved.*

Original Signed
Robt R Daniell
M H Barremore

W. H. Dudley
S. A. Dudley
Peter Wahl
Michael Hahn
Notary Public

I Hereby Certify, the foregoing to be a true copy of the original Act extant and of record in my office: In Faith Whereof I grant these presents, signed by me officially, and bearing the impress of my seal of office, at the City of New Orleans, this first day of November eighteen hundred and fifty nine.

Michael Hahn
Notary Public

STATE OF LOUISIANA, CITY OF NEW ORLEANS.

Be it Known, That on this First day of November in the year of our Lord one thousand eight hundred and fifty nine and of the Independence of the United States of America the eighty fourth Before me, MICHAEL HAHN, A Notary Public, duly commissioned and sworn, in and for the Parish of Orleans, State of Louisiana, and in the presence of the witnesses hereinafter named and undersigned

PERSONALLY CAME AND APPEARED *Uriah H. Dudley* residing in this city who declared that for the consideration, and on the terms and conditions hereinafter expressed, he does by these presents, grant, bargain, sell, convey, transfer, assign, set over and deliver, with all legal warranties, unto *Peter Wahl* also residing in this city here present, accepting and purchasing for *himself his* heirs and assigns, and acknowledging delivery and due possession thereof

A certain negro man slave for life, named "Mercury" now aged about thirty three years.

Being the same slave the present vendor purchased from Sam D Bein, by an act passed before George Ramshido, Notary Public, in this City, on the 14th of April 1853.

The warranty of the present sale extends to title only, and does not include the redhibitory vices, defects and maladies prescribed by law.

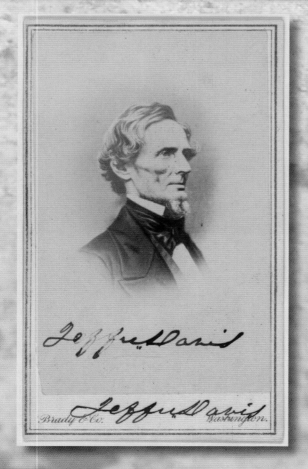

■ ABOVE : A deed of conveyance of slaves (right), which was issued on November 1, 1859, in New Orleans. In the deed, which was certified by the notary Michael Hahn, it is noted that Uriah H. Dudley sells to Peter Wahl the approximately 33-year-old black person named Mercury. The slave has already changed owner in 1853. The deed is laid down that Mercury will remain a slave for life. Also, in the bottom paragraph on the right side it is specified that there is no guarantee for the character and health of the slave. On the left side one can see a contract between spouses, in which the wife relinquishes all rights to the husband.

dependent on slavery had more to do with climate and economy than morality. Many in the South didn't own slaves, either, but they had the American mindset of not liking to be told what to do in their own states.

In the early years of the 19th century, the nation took a middle road, tolerating slavery's existence slavery in all new lands north of 36°30'.

In 1852, abolitionist author Harriet Beecher Stowe gave the anti-slavery (abolition) movement a powerful voice when she published *Uncle Tom's Cabin*, which became a best-seller in the United States and abroad. It was a work of fiction by a woman who knew nothing about the South and spent very little time there, but it played to the politics of abolitionists. In January 1854, Nebraska Territory was split, opening Kansas to the possibility of slavery but keeping Nebraska free in direct violation of the Missouri Compromise, and free-soilers and pro-slavery elements made Kansas a battleground. In 1857, the Supreme Court's Dred Scott decision struck a further blow against abolitionists, stating that a slave did not become a man when he entered a free state, and further asserting that prohibiting slavery's spread was unconstitutional.

Other powerful voices spoke out against slavery, including former slave Frederick Douglass, newspapermen William Lloyd Garrison and Horace Greeley, and Massachusetts Senator Charles Sumner, who was caned on the Senate floor by a South Carolina congressman, Preston Brooks, in 1856, for his fiery condemnation.

As the slavery issue entered the national consciousness, the movement gave rise to a new American political party, the Republicans. In 1860, a Republican, Abraham Lincoln, of Illinois, became the nation's 16th President, a development unsatisfactory to Southerners. Lincoln had not been on the ballot in the South. From a Southern perspective, he had won the Presidency with only 39.8% of the vote. John Breckenridge carried nine of the future 11 Confederate States. The South now had a President that they had not elected. One by one, the Southern states seceded. The stage was set.

Abraham Lincoln

■ ABOVE: **Abraham Lincoln.**
■ OPPOSITE: **Jefferson Davis.**

while trying to limit its spread. This was not easy, because the United States was growing by leaps and bounds, pushing ever westward. The Louisiana Purchase doubled the size of the nation, raising the question of what to do in the new lands. Should they be free, or should each decide its status democratically? The first attempt at controlling the problem came in 1820 with the Missouri Compromise, which prohibited

Chapter Two:
Beginnings

Andrew Jackson

From an original portrait painted from life.

Johnson, Fry & Co. Publishers, New York.

■ **ABOVE:** Andrew Jackson, known also as Old Hickory, 7th President of the United States.

In addition to the slavery issue, the Civil War hinged on the question of states' rights. If a state was to decide it no longer wished to be in the Union, did it have the right to secede? The Southern position was that the Founders had built this concept into the Articles and the Constitution as a check to the power of the Federal government. The idea of nullification and secession had come up before during the Presidency of Andrew Jackson. In 1832, South Carolina objected to a tariff passed by Congress and refused to enforce it, declaring it null and void within the state. President Jackson threatened to hang those who refused to obey the laws, and South Carolina backed down. There remained, however, a feeling in the South that nullification and secession remained viable options if a state felt its rights were being violated by the national government.

In the South, the issue was one of states' rights much more than slavery. On December 20, 1860, South Carolina became the first Southern state to secede from the Union. Soon, others joined it. Since each state asserted its political sovereignty, the states entered into a confederacy, naming themselves the Confederate States of America, and inaugurating a President, Jefferson Davis, in February 1861.

At his own inauguration in March, President Abraham Lincoln stated that he had no wish to invade the South or end slavery, but would protect government property in the South. He held out hope for a peaceful solution to the problem, but rejected Confederate claims that they were a legitimate government.

The first shots of the war were fired on April 12, 1861, at the Union's Fort Sumter, situated on a man-made island in Charleston Harbor. President Lincoln's general in chief, the elderly Winfield Scott, had encouraged Lincoln to abandon the fort, but

Lincoln insisted on keeping it manned and re-supplied. The Confederate batteries shelled the fort, and its commander, Major Robert Anderson, surrendered the following day to General P.G.T. Beauregard, a former student of his at West Point. Two days later, Lincoln issued a proclamation calling for 75,000 volunteers to serve a 90-day term in the army. Nobody knew at the time that the war would drag on for four years and include over 200 named battles.

At the war's outset, the entire Northern Army had only 16,000 men. Initial response to calls for troops

■ **RIGHT: An extract from the** *Charleston Mercury*, **South Carolina, announcing the secession, December 1860.**

■ **BELOW: The bombardment of Fort Sumter, Charleston Harbor, April 12-13, 1861.**

THE

UNION

IS

DISSOLVED!

Passed unanimously at 1.15 o'clock, P. M., December 20th, 1860.

AN ORDINANCE

To dissolve the Union between the State of South Carolina and other States united with her under the compact entitled " The Constitution of the United States of America."

We, the People of the State of South Carolina, in Convention assembled, do declare and ordain, and it is hereby declared and ordained,

That the Ordinance adopted by us in Convention, on the twenty-third day of May, in the year of our Lord one thousand seven hundred and eighty-eight, whereby the Constitution of the United States of America was ratified, and also, all Acts and parts of Acts of the General Assembly of this State, ratifying amendments of the said Constitution, are hereby repealed; and that the union now subsisting between South Carolina and other States, under the name of " The United States of America," is hereby dissolved.

CHARLESTON

MERCURY

EXTRA

was enthusiastic but, as it became apparent that the war would last a while, enlistment fell off. Both sides eventually resorted to the draft by late 1863. Many immigrants enlisted in both armies, and at a much higher rate than native-born Americans. Wages had risen, and the wage for an army private was not terribly competitive. Equipping the troops became a problem for both sides; for example, the North could only produce 5,000 weapons per month, a 10th of the demand, and arms had to be procured from overseas.

Throughout the war, draft evasion and desertion also plagued both armies. In the North, 120,000 men evaded the draft and another 230,000 deserted, as did 100,000 Southerners. In New York, Irish immigrants rioted after finding out that their new citizenship also made them draft-eligible. And a rich man could buy his way out of combat. In the North, a man could hire a proxy for $300 to serve in his place until mid-1864; of the 168,649 drafted in the North, 117,986 sent proxies. Among those doing so were John D. Rockefeller, Andrew Carnegie, J.P. Morgan, and Theodore Roosevelt, Sr. Fraud was also a problem. Some men enlisted multiple times—called "bounty-jumping"—to get the enlistment bonuses.

The Union immediately began a naval blockade to shut down the Confederate economy, but a blockade was difficult because of the sheer length of the Confederate coastline—over 3,500 miles—and the lack of Union naval ships. When the blockade began, the Union Navy had only 16 ships and 1,500 men. By the end of the war, the Union had 626 additional ships and 58,000 men, and had captured 1,149 ships trying to run the blockade, cutting Southern exports by 90%. Southern shipbuilders turned to swift, steam-driven blockade-runners, and came

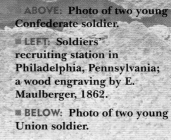

ABOVE: **Photo of two young Confederate soldier.**

■ LEFT: **Soldiers' recruiting station in Philadelphia, Pennsylvania; a wood engraving by E. Maulberger, 1862.**

■ BELOW: **Photo of two young Union soldier.**

up with new offensive weapons including ironclads, ramming ships, and even the world's first successful submarine. In the end, the Union Navy prevailed.

The South faced a grave disadvantage. Most of the nation's industry was located in the North. The North had 110,000 factories employing 1.3 million, the South only 18,000 employing 110,000. Northern factories produced 97% of all firearms. The Gross Domestic Product of just New York State was greater than that of the entire Confederacy in 1860. The North had 31,246 miles of railroad to the South's 9,283, and the South made only 19 of the 470 locomotives produced in 1860. The Southern railroads were also operating on five different gauges of track whereas the Union had a uniform gauge throughout. The North had nearly 21 million people, the South only 9 million, about one-third of whom were slaves. Three Northern states—New York, Pennsylvania, and Massachusetts—had 50,000 more white men of military age than did the entire Confederacy.

The South did have some advantages. First, it would be fighting a defensive war. Second, the South had long bred many of the nation's greatest military minds, giving it a distinct advantage in battle, especially early in the war before the North's great warriors rose through the ranks (25% of the North's officer corps, including General Robert E. Lee, who was offered the command of the army by Lincoln, resigned their commissions to fight for the Confederacy). Lincoln went through one unsuccessful general after another before finally finding successful men such as Ulysses Grant and William T. Sherman.

Two great armies formed, trained, and prepared for battle, though neither had any idea how fierce a war lay ahead, or how long.

■ ABOVE: The sinking of the *Cumberland* by the iron-clad *Merrimac* off Newport News, Virginia, March 8, 1862.

■ LEFT: A Currier and Ives print from a few years after the Civil War shows express trains leaving a station.

Chapter Three:
The Battle is Joined

The first great battle of the Civil War was fought on the lush green meadows of Northern Virginia, not far from the nation's capital. In fact, some Northerners, eager to witness what they felt might be not only the war's beginning but also its end, turned the battle into a festive social event, riding out on horses and buggies to watch the armies. The Union Army was led by the first in the long line of incapable generals, Major General Irvin McDowell, the Confederates by Generals Joseph E. Johnston and P.G.T. Beauregard. Like most Civil War battles, this one is known by two names. The North named battles after natural features such as rivers, while the South named battles after the nearest town. The Battle of Bull Run, as it was known by the North, also called the Battle of Manassas, was fought on July 21, 1861. In the words of General Beauregard: "The political hostilities of a generation were now face to face with weapons instead of words."

Two armies of untrained boys fought it out in the summer heat, the battle further confused by the fact that there were as yet no standardized uniforms and that the flags still looked nearly the same. It wasn't till after the battle that uniforms became more standardized Union blue and Confederate gray or butternut. It was a rout. The Confederates seized 5,000 badly-needed muskets, half a million cartridges, and 28 pieces of artillery. McDowell's plans for a quick march on Richmond were doused when the Union Army turned tail and retreated down the road to Washington—a road clogged by panicked civilians who had come to watch the show.

BELOW: The First Battle of Bull Run.

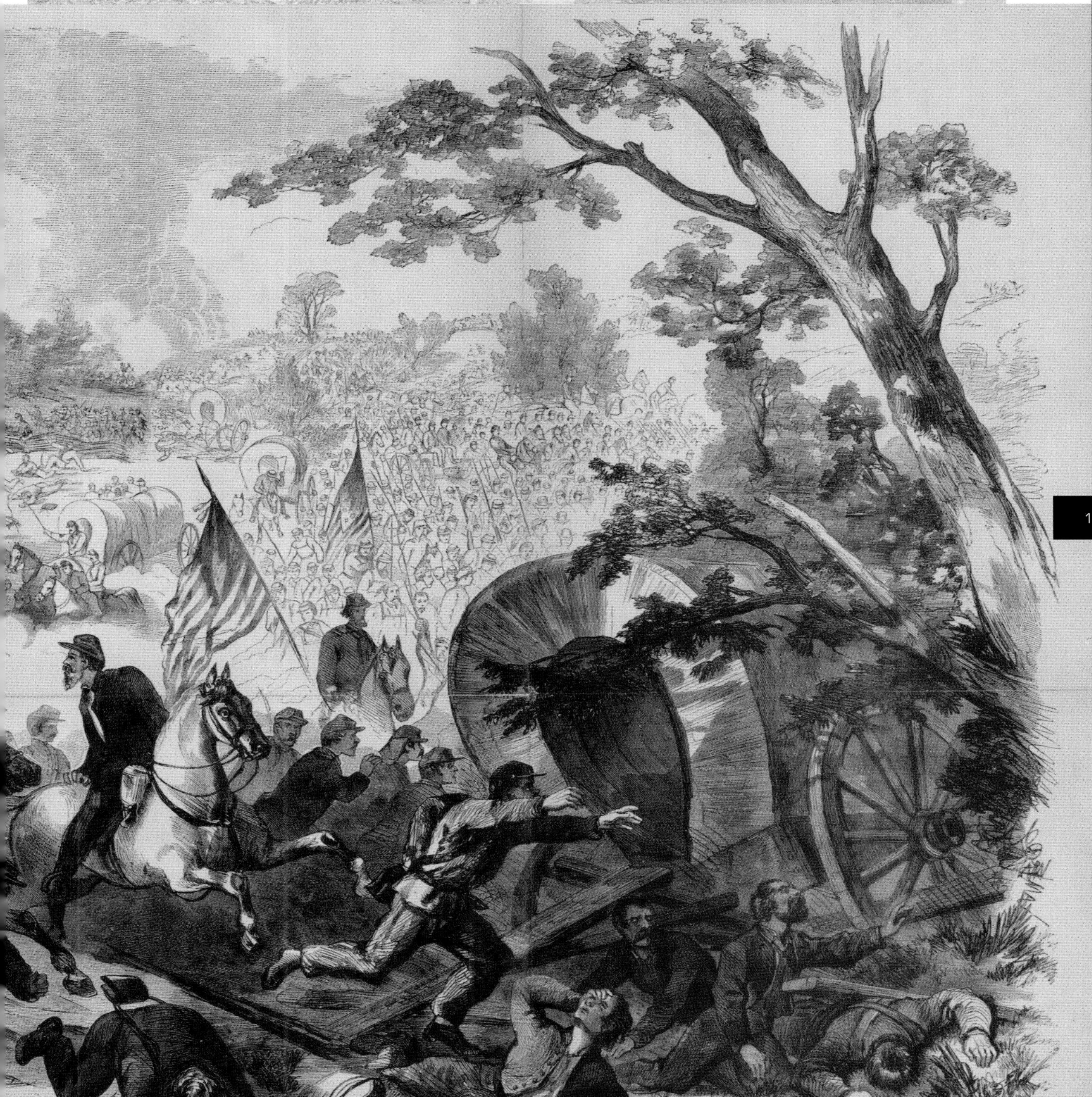

■ ABOVE: Major George B. McClellan and his wife.

The first large battle of the Civil War taught both sides that the war would be bitterly contested and came with the realization that a long war was setting in. The casualties in this first major engagement, 5,200 combined, shocked the nation. Heads of newspapers called for investigations into the terrible bloodletting and demanded that generals be fired because of the death toll. Thirteen months later, on this same battlefield, 23,000 would fall in the Second Battle of Bull Run, but the nation would no longer be shocked. Massive casualties were all too common now.

McDowell was replaced by Major General George B. McClellan, who took command of the Army of the Potomac and instituted a strict training regimen. McClellan thought very highly of himself, but bristled with harsh and condescending criticism for others, including Lincoln, whom he called a "well-intentioned baboon." McClellan promised his men that he would be careful not to shed their blood unnecessarily, and was much loved for it. But, following Manassas, his army lounged around Washington for a full eight months, doing nothing, while the South scrambled to put together the raw materials and men needed for the war. Lincoln grew increasingly exasperated with McClellan. "If McClellan isn't going to use his army," he quipped at one point, "I'd like to borrow it for a while."

By the time McClellan finally moved, there were more than 1 million men at arms, North and South. On April 4, the army of 121,500 men, 14,592 horses, and over 1,000 wagons, embarked in 400 ships to Fort Monroe, on a peninsula southeast of the Confederate capital at Richmond. Once in place, McClellan faced a small force of only 10,000 Confederate troops at Yorktown under Major General Prince John Magruder. Magruder was an expert at putting on musicals and theatrical performances, and at Yorktown he performed his masterpiece: marching his men up over a hill, in clear view of the Federals, and then retracing his steps to the back of the hill—his men continued this charade for hours. McClellan was fooled into thinking that the force was 10 times as large when it was actually one Confederate battalion marching in a continuous circle in front of him. Instead of attacking, McClellan called for reinforcements. He was only 63 miles from Richmond, and would get as close as nine miles at Seven Pines on May 31, when the Union Army could hear Richmond's church bells tolling. Robert E. Lee told President Jefferson Davis that Richmond must not fall. It would mean the war. His Confederate counterpart, General Joseph E. Johnston, remarked that only McClellan would have hesitated to attack in such a superior situation. Lincoln was at his wit's end. "You must attack!" he told his general. McClellan commented acidly to himself that perhaps Lincoln would like to come try it himself. McClellan's own men began to doubt him. One of the nicknames given to him by one-armed General Phillip Kearny was "The Virginia Creeper."

Finally, on May 31, 1862, the armies collided at Seven Pines, Virginia, where the Confederate General Johnston attempted to crush two of McClellan's isolated Corps. The fighting became vicious and lasted for two days after which McClellan pulled his army back to consolidate his lines. The South lost 3,200 men to the North's 2,400, but the biggest loss was to General Johnston—out of the war for eight months with wounds.

Replacing Johnston was General Robert E. Lee. So far in the war Lee had been in minor commands in South Carolina and Western Virginia. Johnston, after hearing that Lee would

22

■ ABOVE: A photo taken shortly after the battle shows the Seven Pines as well as a makeshift memorial.

■ LEFT: Robert E. Lee.

take over his command said, "This was the best wound the South could have, for President Davis has little confidence in me but has elevated someone to command that he has full confidence in."

General Stonewall Jackson and 17,000 men kept three armies larger than his own pinned down in the Shenandoah Valley. Driving his army in marches of up to 36 miles a day, and convinced God was on his side, his actions kept 40,000 Union soldiers from becoming reinforcements for McClellan.

General Lee assumed command, renaming his army the Army of Northern Virginia, and sent his cavalry under J.E.B. Stuart to reconnoiter the Union position. Stuart rode with 1,200 men in a four-day, 100-mile circle around the Union position, reporting to Lee that its flank was unprotected. Lee was now ready to attack. Recalling Stonewall Jackson from the Shenandoah, he prepared to attack McClellan's superior force.

The result was the Seven Days Battles, from June 25 to July 1. All but one were Union victories, and the casualties were huge on both sides. Lee lost 20,000 men, but the numerically superior McClellan retreated. In each day of the Seven Days Battles the Southern forces attacked and drove back the much larger Union Army. Combined losses were 37,000 for this campaign, with Lee's Army of Northern Virginia taking more than 21,000.

With England and France considering recognition of the Confederacy, Lincoln desperately needed a victory or a cause to keep Europe out of the war. On July 22, he announced to his cabinet that he intended to issue a proclamation freeing the slaves, but was convinced to wait until after a Union victory. Though the proclamation would free no slaves, it would signal a change

■ ABOVE:
Thomas Stonewall Jackson.

ABOVE: The Battle of Groveton or Second Bull Run between the Union Army, commanded by General Pope, and the Confederate Army, under General Robert E. Lee. This picture was sketched from Baldface Hill, looking toward the village of Groveton.

BELOW: The dead on the battlefield at Antietam.

in Northern war aims from union to emancipation.

The majority of McClellan's troops were administratively transferred to Major General John Pope's Army of Virginia, who fared no better at the Second Battle of Bull Run on August 29-30 and was subsequently sent packing to put down the Sioux Uprising of 1862 in Minnesota. Lincoln had little trust in McClellan, believing that he had intentionally delayed reinforcements at Bull Run. But he reluctantly admitted he had to fight with the tools he had, no matter how dull, and rehired his nemesis.

In early September, Lee prepared to launch an invasion of the North, possibly drawing border state Maryland to the Confederate cause. At noon on September 13, Corporal Barton Mitchell of the 27th Indiana Regiment discovered three cigars wrapped in paper near Frederick, Maryland. The paper was General Lee's Special Order 191 written out to the division commander, Daniel H. Hill. This order specified the entire marching orders of Lee's men, including how divided the army currently was. McClellan rejoiced at

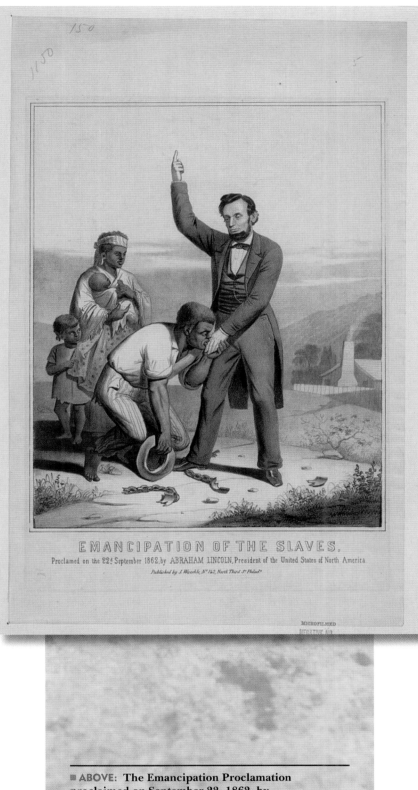

■ ABOVE: **The Emancipation Proclamation proclaimed on September 22, 1862, by Abraham Lincoln.**

■ABOVE: The Battle of Shiloh.

the discovery: "With these orders if I do not whip Bobby Lee I will be willing to go home." But he failed to act on this information for 18 hours. On the 15th, Lee was near Sharpsburg, with the Potomac at his back and the Antietam Creek in front of him. And on the 16th, the forces finally clashed.

Despite a 2-1 advantage and knowledge of Lee's plans, McClellan failed to crush the Confederate Army, refusing to send up 20,000 reserves at a critical moment. Some historians claim that had he pressed the attack, the war would have been over. But instead, he did nothing, and Lee slipped back across the Potomac. The battlefield was littered with the dead in the bloodiest day of the war. Nearly 23,000 men were killed, wounded, or missing. This terrible battle, which lasted less than 10 hours, resulted in one casualty almost every second. A sergeant in the 118th Pennsylvania Regiment wrote this concerning the battle, "For an instant, the entire landscape around me turned red."

General McClellan had been continually on the brink of total victory but had let his doubts about the size of the enemy cow him. His intelligence network estimated the Army of Northern Virginia at over 100,000 when in reality it never concentrated more than 38,000.

Antietam had halted the Confederate offensive into the North and, as a result, Lincoln felt confident enough to issue his Emancipation Proclamation and discourage English and French recognition of the Confederacy. On September 22, Lincoln issued the Proclamation, which freed all slaves in the rebellious states effective January 1, 1863. England and France would not enter into a war over slavery, and even President Jefferson Davis knew that the South now would stand or fall alone.

Lincoln then fired McClellan for his chronic lack of aggressiveness,

admitting, "I have made a grave mistake. Alas, for my poor country." He replaced McClellan with Major General Ambrose Burnside, who led the army long enough to suffer a devastating loss at the Battle of Fredericksburg before being replaced by Major General Joseph Hooker.

The Union fared better out West, thanks to a brilliant, aggressive tactician named Ulysses Grant. The Battle of Shiloh, literally "Place of Peace" in Hebrew, on April 6-7, was little more than an undisciplined brawl between two untrained armies. A heroic stand in a grove of trees, known as the Hornets' Nest, coupled with a fortuitous arrival of Federal reinforcements, snatched victory out of the jaws of defeat for Union forces. The battle also cost the Confederates one of their best generals with the death of Albert Sidney Johnston. Johnston was hit behind the knee and reeled in the saddle, his aide lowering him to the ground. The bleeding could easily have been stopped, but Johnston's surgeon was 200 yards away treating some Union wounded. Instead, Johnston bled to death. It was such a devastating blow that his replacement, General Beauregard, hid the news of Johnston's death to prevent the loss of morale to the men.

■ **ABOVE: A young girl holds a photo of her dead father. Many children were left fatherless during the Civil War.**

■ **RIGHT: Ulysses Grant.**

■ **BELOW: This young soldier, Private Altman, survived the Battle of Shiloh only to die of disease a few weeks later.**

LIEUT. GENERAL U. S. GRANT.

Shiloh was a bloodbath, with 2,477 dead and 23,000 total casualties—more casualties in one battle than the United States had suffered in all its previous wars and as many as Waterloo. Grant commented that the dead were so thick on the field that a man could walk from one end to the other without ever stepping on the ground.

Grant was relieved of command after Shiloh, a victim of General Halleck's jealousy (Halleck accused him of being drunk during the battle) and had to be talked out of quitting by his friend General Sherman. He would be back. Lincoln had at last found his general, saying admiringly, "I can't spare this man. He fights." Within three months Grant was again in charge of the Federal Army of the Tennessee.

The war in the West focused on control of America's interior artery, the mighty Mississippi River. This river played a huge role in the economy of the South as it provided for the primary transportation for 1,000 miles, allowing goods and men to travel. One Southern city after another fell to Union forces. Under a reinstated General Grant, the Union won victories in Missouri and Kentucky, and reclaimed Tennessee

■ **BELOW: The splendid naval triumph on the Mississippi, April 24, 1862. Destruction of the rebel gunboats, rams, and iron-clad batteries by the Union Fleet under Flag Officer Farragut.**

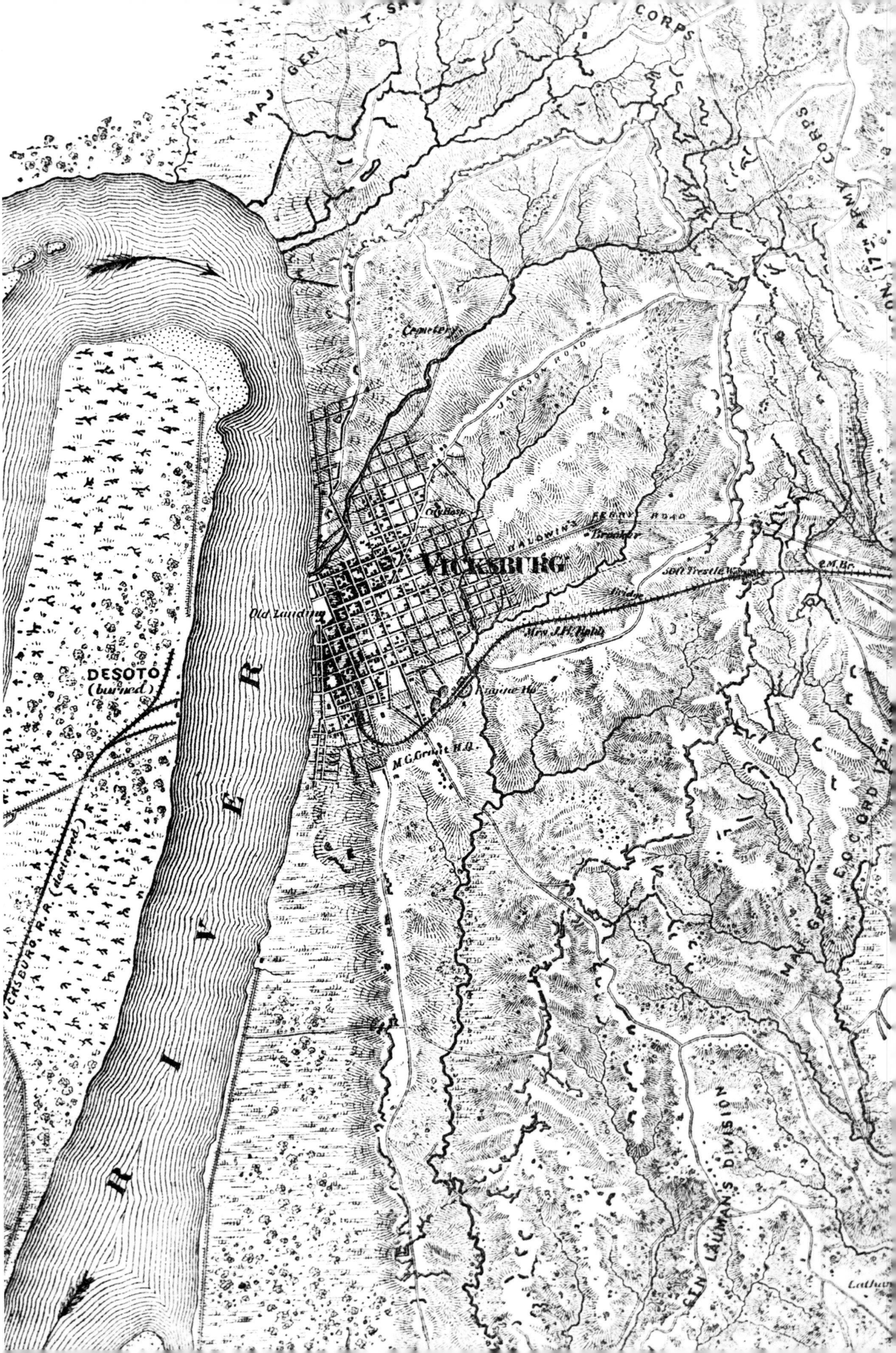

DESOTO
(burned)

VICKSBURG

Old Landing

Cemetery

JACKSON ROAD

FERRY ROAD

BALDWIN'S

Bridge

Mrs. J.H. Flint

Ravine Rd

M.G.Grant H.Q.

Soft Trestle Bridge

C.M.Rd.

MAJ. GEN. W.T. SHERMAN'S CORPS

CORPS

ARMY CORPS

MAJ. GEN. McCLERNAND'S

GEN. LAUMAN'S DIVISION

HARPER'S WEEKLY.

A JOURNAL OF CIVILIZATION

Vol. VII—No. 349.] NEW YORK, SATURDAY, SEPTEMBER 5, 1863. [SINGLE COPIES SIX CENTS.

MOSBY'S GUERILLAS DESTROYING SUTLERS' TRAIN.—[See Page 567.]

■ ABOVE: The title page of *Harper's Weekly*, September 5, 1863, showing Mosby's Raiders destroying a sutler's train.

■ OPPOSITE: An 1863 map showing the plan of the Siege of Vicksburg.

in 1862. In April, Navy Flag Officer David Farragut, commander of the West Gulf Blockading Squadron, ran his force up the Mississippi to New Orleans, splitting the Confederacy in two and becoming the first navy officer to become an admiral.

Soon, the only remaining Confederate stronghold was the city of Vicksburg. Vicksburg, perched on a high bluff, was called "the nail that holds the South's two halves together" by President Jefferson Davis.

A prolonged 48-day siege at Vicksburg ended with its surrender on July 4, 1863. The Federals now commanded the great river, and the ability of the Confederates to use the river as a highway was gone forever. The fall of Vicksburg may have had the greatest impact upon the war. Over 38,000 Southern soldiers surrendered along with the capture of 140 cannon and 1,000 horses. Vicksburg was Grant's crowning achievement and higher commands now awaited him.

The city of Vicksburg did not celebrate the Fourth of July for 82 years. Not until the end of World War Two did this great city again look upon the Fourth as a day of Independence.

Lincoln was certain now. "Grant is my man and I am his for the rest of the war," he stated emphatically. Grant had the Confederates on the run in the West.

Guerilla fighters and raiders played an important role in the war, especially in the West. The most famous is arguably Confederate cavalry Colonel John Mosby, commander of the 43rd Battalion Virginia Cavalry, and better known as "Mosby's Raiders." Mosby and his men launched lightning raids and reconnaissance missions behind enemy lines in Northern Virginia and the Shenandoah Valley, not far from Washington. Most of the raids were made by 20 to 80 men,

THE RUINS OF LAWRENCE, KANSAS.—Sketched by a Corresp

who struck and then disappeared like ghosts, leading to Mosby's nickname, "The Gray Ghost." Mosby was proud of his role, stating, "It is just as legitimate to fight an enemy in the rear as in the front. The only difference is in the danger..." By some accounts, Mosby and his small band were responsible for the capture, death, or wounding of 1,200 Union soldiers. Mosby was the one man mentioned in General Lee's reports more than any other commander.

Out West, the main guerilla actions took place in Missouri. One band, Quantrill's Raiders, led by William Quantrill, attacked the Free-Soil

■ **LEFT: The ruins of buildings in Lawrence, Kansas, following the attack by William Quantrill and his Confederate raiders, Woodcut, c. 1863.**

town of Lawrence, Kansas, in August 1863, ordered to kill every man and burn every house. By the time they were done, 182 men and boys lay dead and 185 buildings had been burned. Some partisan bands caused enough problems to necessitate the use of the Union Army to quell them. A few Native American tribes were involved in the war, the most famous being Cherokee Confederate Brigadier General Stand Watie.

Chapter Four:
Billy Yank and Johnny Reb

■ **ABOVE: An unknown Union cavalryman.**

According to Ken Burns in his acclaimed Civil War miniseries, the typical Civil War soldier was 5'8" and 143 pounds. His average age was 25 and, though the minimum age for enlistment was 18, there were many boys under 18 in both armies. In the Union Army alone, there were 100,000 boys below the age of 15, and it was not uncommon for drummer boys to be nine or 10. A soldier had a one in 65 chance of dying in the war, and his chances of being wounded were one in 10. His chances of dying of disease were one in 13. Soldiers came from all walks of life. They were farmers, factory workers, and many Northern soldiers were immigrants, particularly Irish and German.

As is still the case, actual enlistment, training, and service proved to be less glamorous than depicted in the recruiting posters. Warren Goss was a young private in the Second Massachusetts Infantry. He found all the claims of the posters to be false save one—chances for travel.

"My first uniform was a bad fit," he writes. "My trousers were too long by three or four inches; the flannel shirt was coarse and unpleasant— too large in the neck and too short elsewhere. The forage cap was an ungainly bag with a pasteboard top and leather visor; the blouse was the only part which seemed decent; while the overcoat made me feel like a little nib of corn amid a preponderance of husk."

For most Civil War soldiers the war was a seemingly endless string of boring days, repetitive routines of camp life, and winter quarters punctuated by a few days of vicious combat. Many times the soldiers of both sides encamped close to one another allowing for fraternization between the men. Throughout the war it was common for front line men on picket duty to strike up

■ **ABOVE: A young Confederate soldier in the uniform of a second lieutenant.**

■ **BELOW: A Federal camp.**

conversations with enemy pickets leading to small unit cease fires. During these times the men often bartered and traded items with enemy soldiers. The most commonly traded items were Southern tobacco for Northern coffee.

Organization of the armies was very similar as their officers were usually trained at the United States Military Academy at West Point, New York. The basic unit of the individual soldier was the regiment. The regiment had a strength of 1,000 men and 40 officers. Each regiment was raised locally and had a distinctive state flair. The regiment had its own state and national colors that they proudly carried and protected. These units adorned their flag with the names of engagements. Each regiment, being raised locally, had men that certainly knew each other. The idea that the Civil War was a war of brother against brother did occur but rarely. The better thought was the war was a war of brother alongside brother, or father, uncle, neighbor, and friend. This was all well and good for morale but when a regiment got in a tight spot, such as the Hornets' Nest at Shiloh, the loss to the local area back home could be devastating. Many a town or village lost a whole generation of young men.

Possibly the worst example of this loss to a small area is the 26th North Carolina Regiment at Gettysburg. This regiment brought 840 men to Gettysburg but by the time it marched home, defeated, beginning on July 5, 1863, only 87 men remained in the regiment. This loss of almost 90% is the highest of any single regiment from either side.

The regimental strength of 1,000 was seldom actually seen on the battlefield. Because of casualties, disease, and straggling, most veteran regiments went into battle with between 300-400 men. At Gettysburg the 69th New York, part of the famed

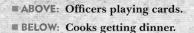

■ ABOVE: **Officers playing cards.**
■ BELOW: **Cooks getting dinner.**

Irish Brigade, marched into battle with only 83 men.

Each regiment was formed into units of three to four to make a brigade. The brigade was the chess piece to the generals. These were the units that the generals incorporated into their tactics. Many brigades were formed of regiments from the same state in the Southern Army.

Three to five brigades would be formed into a division commanded by a major general. Confederate Divisions would have 6,000 to 8,000 men. Federal Divisions usually had 3,000 to 4,000 men. The division was then formed into the Corps commanded by a major general in the Federal Army and a lieutenant general in the Southern Army.

The vast majority of Civil War battles were fought on Southern soil, as the Federals Armies were usually the aggressor. The greatest number of engagements during the war occurred in Virginia, with 122 named battles. Tennessee had the second most battles with 38, and Mississippi was third with 34. Along with each of these major battles were literally hundreds of small engagements that always took the lives or health of some of the men involved. The most northern battle of the war occurred in St. Albans, Vermont, just 15 miles from the Canadian border. The most westerly battle was at Picacho Pass in Arizona.

Identification of the dead and wounded was a major problem during the war. No formal "Dog Tags" were used by the individual soldier. Men hoped that after a battle, if they were killed, the men of their regiment would identify their bodies so a name could be inscribed upon the headstone and the family informed. By 1863, men began knitting their names with thread into the back of their jackets to help with identification. Individual states also began to issue specific

■ **LEFT:** An African-American soldier and his family.

BELOW: A dead Confederate soldier on May 19, 1864, at Spotsylvania Courthouse.

38

buttons and identifying features upon their uniforms, which aided in identification. Even with some care to identify soldiers killed in action the number of "unknown dead" remained high. At Gettysburg National Cemetery there are 3,600 men buried there just from the Northern Army. Of these, 979 are completely unknown with an additional 425 unknown but identified by a state marking. More than 3,200 Confederate soldiers from this battle were disinterred from the fields of Gettysburg and taken home to Hollywood Cemetery in Richmond as complete unknowns.

The most important piece of equipment for the infantryman was his boots, and it was inevitable that the infantry was issued the poorest ones. These leather boots came in two or three sizes and did not differentiate between left and right, requiring the men to adjust them using extra socks. Each man also carried his musket and accoutrements, 40 rounds of ammunition in his cartridge box, and 160 more in his pockets, knapsack, or haversack. His blanket and light

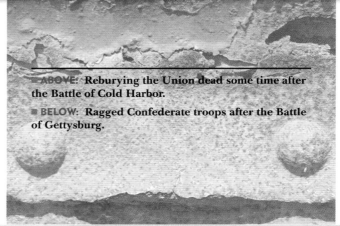

■ ABOVE: **Reburying the Union dead some time after the Battle of Cold Harbor.**

■ BELOW: **Ragged Confederate troops after the Battle of Gettysburg.**

■ ABOVE: A Union uniform.

rubber blanket were made into a bedroll, the ends tied together, and worn over the shoulder. The roll usually contained an extra shirt, a pair of socks, and a half-section of "dog-tent" which, when buttoned to the half carried by a comrade, made a very fair shelter for two men. The provision issued to a soldier was a much-abridged ration, but it brought up the total weight of his burden to a good 30 pounds or more to carry for days at a time, in all weather, over all kinds of roads. He also carried a spoon-fork or spoon-knife combination, a canteen (which was usually discarded as too heavy in favor of a tin cup), possibly a tin plate, matches, a pipe, and tobacco. His belt had a small pouch for percussion caps, a sling from which to hang the scabbard of his bayonet, and a leather cartridge box with tools to clean his rifle.

Topping off the load was the haversack, made of either canvas or oilcloth and worn over the shoulder. One soldier described his as his "odorous haversack, which often stinks with a mixture of bacon, salt pork, junk, sugar, coffee, tea, desiccated vegetables, rice, bits of yesterday's dinner, and old scraps."

Confederate soldiers were less well supplied, often wearing whatever clothes they could find. However, they were somewhat better equipped than popular myth would have us believe. As late as the Siege of Petersburg and the Appomattox Campaign, Confederates were issued new uniforms, usually the Richmond Depot shell jackets.

The infantry was expected to be able to march many miles a day, sometimes for a number of days in a row. The men were lean from the walking and toting. Many carried a small glass daguerreotype photograph of a wife or loved one in a small frame with a clasp, which they would look at when times got rough and they dreamed of home.

■ **ABOVE: Soldiers on both sides kept glass photos of loved ones inside wooden and leather cases like this one.**

■ **OPPOSITE ABOVE: A very young Samuel W. Doble of Company D, 12ᵗʰ Maine Infantry Regiment, with his drum. This photo is an ambrotype by Sewell Shattuck and is hand-colored.**

■ **OPPOSITE: Dreaming of home.**

THE SOLDIER'S DREAM OF HOME.

Chapter Five:
Technology

The Civil War was the first modern industrial war. Men fought using Napoleonic tactics against weapons and machines unimaginable a few decades earlier. These included the first railroad artillery, land mines, and telescopic sights. In all, 243 military patents were issued in 1862 alone. The sheer destructiveness of these modern weapons, combined with the rudimentary medical care available to treat not only wounds but also disease, resulted in astronomical casualty rates on both sides.

The infantryman's standard weapon, the single-shot musket, had been replaced by rifles, which had helical grooves inside the barrel that spun the bullet as it traveled down the barrel, improving its aerodynamics and accuracy. Rifles were improved when a French Army officer named Claude Minié invented a one-inch-long slug that was smaller than the barrel, allowing it to be loaded with minimal effort. The rifle and Minié ball could kill at up to 1,000 yards, and was deadly accurate to 200 yards. The self-contained bullet with powder also increased the speed at which a rifle could be loaded. In the day of smooth bore muzzle loaders the rate of fire was barely more than one round per minute. By the Civil War, a veteran soldier with a rifled musket could arm and fire close to four times a minute. Tactics and technology had truly changed. Less than 30 years prior to the war the grand infantry strategy was to mass one's infantry close to the enemy lines, fire a volley, and then charge to close with the bayonet. Some officers—and the men they commanded—would find out the hard way that this method no longer worked against modern weaponry. Massed infantry charges continued into late 1864, resulting in casualties of epic numbers. At the Battle of Franklin, the South lost 12,000 men in less than an hour upon their charge. On July 1,

■ **ABOVE:** Assorted Minié balls.

■ **BELOW:** The patent design for the Minié ball, Harpers Ferry, Virginia.

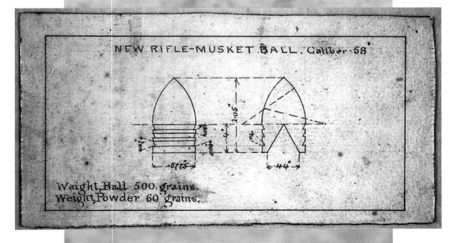

NEW RIFLE-MUSKET BALL. Caliber .58

Weight, Ball 500 grains.
Weight, Powder 60 grains.

1864, at Cold Harbor, General Grant lost 7,000 men in 20 minutes, and regretted it for the rest of his life.

Another development in firearms was the Spencer repeating rifle, capable of firing more than one shot without having to reload. In fact, a Spencer could fire seven shots in half a minute without reloading—giving those using it a distinct advantage. The Spencer gave the Union a technological edge, as most Confederates never had access to a repeating rifle.

The Civil War was also one of the first wars in which aircraft were used. A good 50 years before powered flight, the hydrogen balloon was used for aerial reconnaissance. Doctor Thaddeus Lowe developed a patented procedure for producing hydrogen gas from zinc and sulfuric acid and collecting the gas in a balloon capable of lifting a couple of men, along with a telegraph key and wire or semaphore flags for signaling. This use of aerial reconnaissance provided the Federal Army with a tremendous advantage.

The Confederates used stationary torpedoes to sink 43 Union vessels. A 40-foot submarine, named CSS *Hunley*, constructed from an old locomotive boiler, became the first submarine to sink an enemy ship. Initial test-dives failed, killing those on board including the inventor, Horace Hunley. Despite this shaky record, a crew volunteered to man her and, on the night of February 17, 1864, the *Hunley*, armed with a spar torpedo, rammed the USS *Housatonic*, sinking her. Unfortunately, the *Hunley* also sank with all hands. In another advance in naval warfare, "ironclad" warships repelled cannonballs that would have sunk a traditional wooden ship. On March 8-9, 1862, the Union ironclad *Monitor* and the Confederate ironclad *Merrimac*, renamed the *Virginia*, fought a classic duel at Hampton Roads, Virginia. At

■ ABOVE: **Women making bullets.**

■ BELOW: **A Spencer repeating rifle.**

■ BOTTOM: **Maine skirmishers with Spencer repeating rifles.**

#165 - 1865 Spencer Rifle, .56-50

that instant, these ironclad warships made every other vessel in the world obsolete. The battle ended in a draw but the age of wooden fighting ships was over.

The telegraph allowed for fast long-distance communication. In 1861, the US Military Telegraph Service was created, manned by civilian operators. In fact, Lincoln had his own telegraph office in the White House, where he could maintain communication with his commanders. By 1862, the Union had 4,000 miles of telegraph wire and over a million messages were sent. In 1864, General Grant was able to stay in constant touch with the President and with his subordinates using the telegraph during the Siege of Petersburg. The telegraph was used to a lesser extent by the Confederacy.

The North's standard-gauge railroad bed, with a distance between the tracks of 4'8½", gave it a huge advantage over the South, which used multiple gauges, as mentioned before.

Another relatively new piece of technology, unrelated to the actual destruction of the enemy, was

the camera. Though still bulky, it allowed anyone to witness scenes that heretofore would have only been relegated to words or drawings. Some photographers, such as Matthew Brady, elevated war photography to an art form. His exhibition in New York City in October 1862, entitled "The Dead of Antietam," brought the war home to the civilian public accustomed only to reading about the war in the newspaper, and his

■ **TOP: Thaddeus Lowe in his balloon at Fair Oaks.**
■ **ABOVE: Thaddeus Lowe's balloon at Gaines' Mill.**
■ **BELOW: The Confederate submarine *Hunley*.**

Fɪɢ. 149. — Le *David* de Hunley.

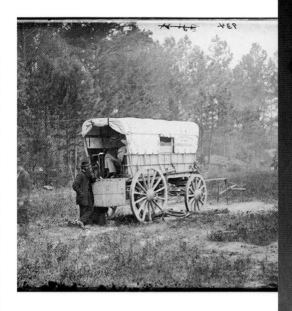

stark, haunting images give modern viewers a glimpse into the realities of this long-ago war. It was common to see horse-drawn wagons advertising photography studios following every

army by 1863. Besides Matthew Brady, the most famous photographer of the war, Alexander Gardner and Timothy O'Sullivan became common names in this new industry.

Chapter Six:
Bitter War

"Who Would Be Free, Themselves Must Strike the Blow!"

$200 $200

COLORED MEN
Of Burlington Co.,

Your Country calls you to the Field of Martial Glory. Providence has offered you an opportunity to vindicate the Patriotism and Manhood of your Race. Some of your brothers accepting this offer on many a well-fought field, have written their names on history's immortal page amongst the bravest of the brave.

NOW IS YOUR TIME!

Remember, that every blow you strike at the call of your Government against this accursed Slaveholders' Rebellion, you Break the Shackles from the Limbs of your Kindred and their Wives and Children.

The Board of Freeholders of Burlington Co.

Now offers to every Able-Bodied COLORED MAN who volunteers in the Service of his Country a BOUNTY of

$200 CASH! $200
WHEN SWORN INTO THE SERVICE, and
$10 PER MONTH
WHILE IN SUCH SERVICE.   COME ONE!   COME ALL!

GEO. SNYDER,
Recruiting Agent for Colored Volunteers of Burlington County.

U. S. Steam Print, Ledger Buildings, Philada.

Poster for Recruitment of Colored Soldiers

■ ABOVE: An African-American recruiting poster.

No one really expected the war to drag on as it did. The first enlistments in both armies were for only 90 days and these troops affectionately referred to themselves as "The 90 Day Wonders." Enlistments ran out and many men went home to their farms or jobs in the North; however, most Confederates were there for the duration. This was especially devastating in the South, with its dearth of manpower. President Jefferson Davis took swift action to keep troops in the field, extending all enlistments for the duration of the war. In a move that angered many common Southerners, he also announced that all able-bodied men would now have to serve three years in the Confederate military, but exempted those men who oversaw more than 20 slaves. This caused many a poor soldier on both sides to conclude that it was a rich man's war, but a poor man's fight. Fully one-half of all eligible Southern males evaded the draft call.

In the North, the first calls for the draft were met with massive riots and inner-city destructions. The draft riots in New York City caused the death of 180 individuals. Eventually, the North brought in veteran infantry regiments to quell the riots.

January 1, 1863, marked the day that all slaves in the South were freed; however, the Emancipation Proclamation carried little weight among Southerners. It was an important propaganda tool and was celebrated by African-Americans and abolitionists. Many African-Americans joined the Union cause. In all, nearly 200,000 served in the Union Army, and 38,000 paid the ultimate price.

At Chancellorsville, the Confederate Army defeated its Union counterpart in a bloody slugfest. Total casualties were around 30,000. By this time, the war had become a war of attrition. The North, with its higher population, could replace soldiers in

■ **ABOVE: A poignant yet terrifying shot shows battered trees and men near Culp's Hill at Gettysburg.**

■ **RIGHT: The Snodgrass House, Chickamauga battlefield, taken in 1902.**

■ **BELOW: The arrival of General Longstreet at General Bragg's headquarters prior to the Battle of Chickamauga.**

the field more easily than the South, especially after Grant cancelled the prisoner exchange policy in 1864. In addition, the North had by now significant advantages in weaponry, transportation, and supplies for the men in the field. Some Confederate soldiers no longer had shoes on their feet, their diets were limited, and their clothing and rifles needed replacement.

Lee now launched a bold offensive into the North once again, driving down the Shenandoah Valley into Pennsylvania. Concurrently, the ineffective Union General Hooker was replaced with the goggle-eyed 47-year-old General George Gordon Meade, who would prove that he was up to the task of facing Lee. Though Lee's trusted subordinate, General Longstreet, warned Lee not to engage the Union force at Gettysburg, Lee, perhaps overconfident, violated his own rules of engagement and attacked. For three days, some of the fiercest fighting of the war raged around the tiny Pennsylvania hamlet as Lee tried to punch a hole through the Union center and gain the high ground. A force under General Pickett, made up of Longstreet's I Corps, made a gallant but unsuccessful charge into the Union lines. The repulse of the charge

may have been one of the war's main turning points. In the end, the Union held, forcing Lee to retreat with his army back to Virginia.

In the West, things were going badly for the Confederates; General Braxton Bragg moved the Army of Mississippi to Chattanooga, Tennessee, and prepared to take Kentucky. This campaign ended in defeat, though the Union General Buell lost his job to General William S. Rosecrans. On December 31, Rosecrans attacked Bragg at Stones River in Murfreesboro, Tennessee. By January 2, 1863, it was apparent that

the battle had become a stalemate and Bragg withdrew his forces. Union and Confederate losses were high; out of the roughly 60,000 soldiers engaged, nearly 23,500 were casualties. Later that same month, Grant took the last Confederate citadel on the Mississippi at Vicksburg, and both the Eastern and Western theaters had turned entirely in favor of the Union. The Confederates managed a victory at Chickamauga, Georgia, in September, and Grant then received needed reinforcements, which resulted in a victory at Chattanooga, Tennessee, in November.

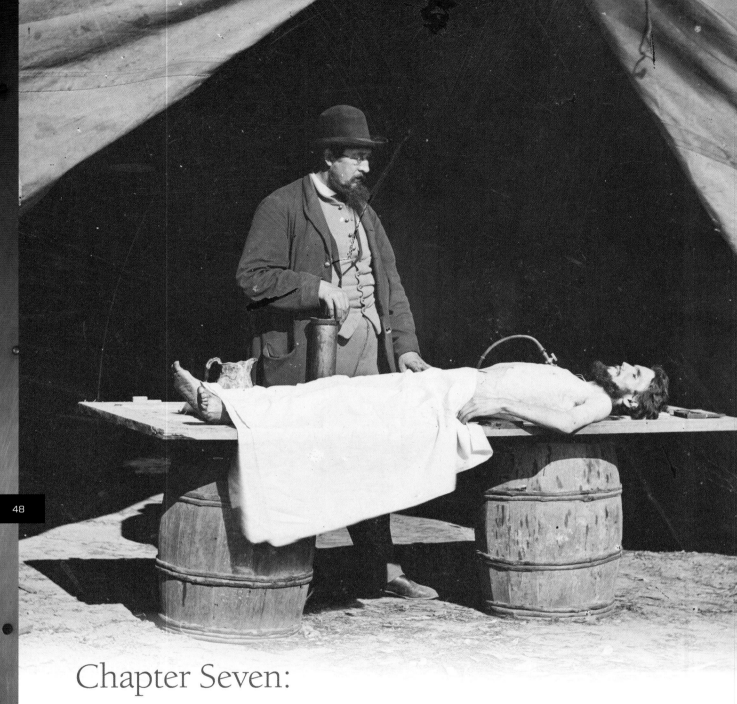

Chapter Seven:

Casualties

■ ABOVE: An enbalmer prepares a dead soldier for the trip back home for burial.

Approximately 2.5% of the American population died in the Civil War. A soldier was less likely to die from a bullet than from a germ; twice as many men died of disease as were killed in combat; 40% of those who died in the war were never identified, though over 100,000 Union corpses were recovered in the South in the three years after the war by details sent to locate and bury uniform-wearing Union skeletons in bramble thickets and open meadows.

The number of Union soldiers killed in action or mortally wounded was 110,100. Total casualties for all reasons were 664,928, with 275,175 wounded in action. The number of Confederates soldiers killed in action or mortally wounded was 94,000, with total deaths at 289,000. 194,026 were wounded in action.

One Union Army surgeon declared that the Civil War was fought "at the end of the medical Middle Ages," and this proved to be true. Conditions in American hospitals at the time were basic at best, and most wounded soldiers were treated in hastily constructed tent-hospitals by under-trained, over-worked army surgeons. Most American doctors were not products of medical schools, but had

Photographed according to Act of Congress, in the year 1862, by Gardner & Gibson, in the Clerk's Office of the District Court of the District of Columbia.

■ **ABOVE:** A stereograph slide shows the terrible result of a direct hit by artillery upon a young Confederate soldier at Gettysburg.

■ **BELOW:** A surgeon's amputation kit.

served apprenticeships under other doctors. American medical schools lagged behind European ones. A US medical degree was two years, compared to four in Europe.

At the outset of the Civil War, neither side had enough doctors to treat the wounded. A small cadre of doctors and nurses, some of whom were volunteers, treated over 10 million cases of injury or sickness during the war. Approximately 200,000 Union and Confederates died of battle wounds. Wounded men were first taken to a field hospital, where they were triaged, often lying on the ground for hours in all weather waiting for treatment. The medical goal was to treat the wounded within 48 hours. When a man was sufficiently stabilized, he was then moved to a permanent military hospital, a grueling wagon trip.

Because of the close proximity of combat, and the effectiveness of modern weaponry, the wounds suffered were horrible. Civil War bullets, made of soft lead, in large .58 caliber fired at a low muzzle velocity, expanded upon hitting the body, resulting in gaping wounds, destroying internal organs and

shattering bones like matchsticks. A head or abdominal wound was a death sentence; a wound to an arm or leg often shattered the bones, requiring amputation. Civil War surgeons and their assistants dealt with one trauma case after another, often for several days at a time, after a large battle.

Surgeons worked at chest-high tables, stripped to the waist and smeared in blood, sawing through mangled limbs as fast as possible as men screamed, then tossing the amputated part onto a pile on the floor. Most operations, but not all, were done while the soldier was under the influence of chloroform.

A soldier now had to fight his second battle, that of disease. Most equipment used in saving a patient

■ ABOVE: A war artist's sketch of a field hospital during the Battle of Chancellorsville.

■ OPPOSITE ABOVE: A surgeon performs a battlefield amputation.

■ OPPOSITE: A double-amputee in a Union hospital, 1865.

was not sterilized, either because there was no time or because of lack of knowledge. Lack of water meant hands were often dirty for days at a time. The most common infections were strep-related bacterial infections, resulting in build-ups of festering pus, and then human flesh began to die and rot as gangrene set in.

Men died from typhoid fever and dysentery caused by poor camp sanitation. Diseases spread rapidly in these days before immunization, with whole camps getting measles, mumps, tuberculosis, or other common ailments. Almost every man in the Union Army suffered from chronic diarrhea or dysentery. In swampy areas, mosquitoes brought not just constant discomfort but malaria.

Calvin Bates.

Chapter Eight:
Prisoners of War

■ ABOVE: A bird's-eye view of Andersonville Prison from the southeast. The print shows Andersonville Prison with the vast prison area surrounded by stockade fences and several banks of cannons in the foreground and the distance.

Over 400,000 soldiers became prisoners of war during the Civil War and 56,000 of them died in prison—a casualty rate twice that of combat. 15.5% of Union prisoners died while incarcerated, as did 12% of Confederates. This high casualty rate was the result of lack of knowledge and poor sanitation rather than a deliberate act on either side. For example, Colonel Hoffman at Elmira Prison put his prisoners on bread and water to save money, resulting in scurvy and death with the resulting lack of meat and vegetables in the prisoners' diets. The most infamous prison of the Civil War, the South's Andersonville, had a 29% mortality rate. The worst Union prison, Camp Douglas in Chicago, had the highest single-month casualty rate of the war when 387 out of 3,884 men perished in February 1863. In all, there were 150 prisons, North and South, of varying quality. Some were in forts or other buildings, but others, out of necessity, were little better than open stockyards where the men had to fend for their own shelter. At Andersonville, 33,000 men were crammed into just over 26 acres of mud and open sewer. Andersonville's main water

source was a sewage-clogged stream, where men waited day and night to draw water—water that was teeming with maggots. Prison diets were unbalanced, with little if any fresh vegetables or fruit, resulting in scurvy. Disease ran rampant. Rats were everywhere. Many prisoners simply lost the will to live under such conditions and let themselves pass away. Young New Jersey prisoner Corporal Charles Hopkins wrote: "The cases of insanity were numerous. Men, strong in mentality, heart, and hope were in a few short months… reduced to imbeciles and maniacs." (Smithsonian, 258)

After the war, Confederate prisoners had to take a loyalty oath to the Union and were then sent home by train. The camp commander at Andersonville, Henry Wirz, was tried in military court for "impairing the health and destroying the lives of prisoners" and was hanged in November 1865 as a war criminal. Interestingly, Elmira's Colonel Hoffman was given a new assignment at Fort Leavenworth. The poor treatment of Union prisoners at Andersonville caused so much ill will in the North that it helped fuel anti-Southern sentiments during Reconstruction.

■ RIGHT: **Federal prisoners undergo awful hardships at Andersonville, where they have to endure the cold and the rain with scarcely enough clothing or shelter.**

Chapter Nine:
The End

In March, Lincoln put his man Grant in charge of all the Union armies, and Grant's friend General William Sherman was given the reins of the Western Army. Grant took the helm of the Army of the Potomac and told Meade to take the war right at Lee and the Confederates, telling Meade "Wherever Lee goes, you will go there also." Each battle was heavily contested, with staggering losses on both sides, but the Union was now seeing the advantage of its large population and could more easily replace those men who fell. Union troops were also better fed, better clothed, and better armed. At the Battle of the Wilderness and Spotsylvania in May, and at Cold Harbor and Petersburg in June, Grant had the Confederates on the defensive and didn't let up.

Meanwhile, Sherman had matters at hand in the West, marching South, taking Atlanta in the summer and then beginning a "March to the Sea" through Georgia. Sherman then took Columbia and Charleston, South Carolina, in February before marching up into North Carolina by April 1865.

On April 2-3, Lee's forces evacuated the capital of the Confederacy at Richmond and Petersburg, and after being doggedly pursued by Grant and Meade, finally surrendered on April 9, at Appomattox Court House, Virginia.

■ BELOW: General Lee surrenders to General Grant at Appomattox Court House.

THE SURRENDER OF LEE.

Chapter Ten:
The Cost of War

Though the monetary cost of the war is in itself huge, it is the human cost that almost defies the imagination. 620,000 soldiers died in the war, in combat or by disease, though some modern historians have suggested the number may be substantially higher. More young men were killed in the Civil War than in all other wars the United States has fought, before or since, combined. Hundreds of thousands of men were wounded, with 60,000 losing a limb. The war virtually bankrupted the South. Two-thirds of her wealth disappeared, much of it with the emancipation of the slaves. Half its farms were in ruins and hundreds of miles of railroads; 40% of all Southern livestock had been confiscated by the armies. Inflation in the South hit 9,000%.

The economic disparity between North and South increased after the war, and unscrupulous speculators from the North reaped profits at the expense of the Southern landowners. The cotton industry revived, soon exceeding its prewar levels. The former slaves continued to till the fields and harvest the cotton, only as paid employees. But the African-American in the South, though he was now free, still had a long way to go to become equal—his struggle for equality would not be fulfilled for another hundred years. In early 1865, General William T. Sherman had granted more than 100,000 African-American families 40 acres of confiscated land, and in some cases a mule to work it, but Lincoln's successor, President Andrew Johnson, reversed this decision, leading to much bitterness from former slaves who felt betrayed by

■ ABOVE: An engraving idealizes a happy return for a wounded veteran to his family.

■ BELOW: The destruction of Richmond.

■ **ABOVE: General Sherman at Atlanta.**

■ **RIGHT: A photo of a sharecropper's house near Greenville, Alabama. This could have been taken right after the Civil War but, in fact, was taken in the 1960s.**

the government that had fought to free them. Since most freed slaves were denied land of their own, they ended up working the land of others, often as "sharecroppers," splitting their crop with the absentee owner. Sharecropping led to an endless cycle of poverty and debt, made worse by bad crop years.

African-Americans made gains in education after the war, aided by 3,000 so-called Freedmen's Schools. By 1900, the literacy rate among African-Americans had risen from 10% to 50%. By the 1880s, most Southern states had introduced "Jim Crow Laws" designed to limit the freedom given African-Americans. The laws led to a deeply segregated society, in which separate most definitely was not equal. In some areas, African-Americans were kept subordinate through the use of

fear, intimidation, and violence; the white-robed Ku Klux Klan formed in 1866 to protect Southern Democratic interests against Northern Republican usurpers but became, in some areas, a terrorist organization.

Reconstruction was a failure, hijacked by Radical Republicans, who disenfranchised most white Southerners, and falling prey to carpetbaggers and profiteers. It ended with the election of 1876, when a deal was cut allowing Rutherford B. Hayes the Presidency in exchange for pulling Federal troops out of the South. Though Southern Democrats promised to respect the voting rights of African-Americans, by the turn of the century, most Southern African-Americans had been disenfranchised.

In the North, the war only temporarily slowed the economy.

The war had been funded by increased taxes and bond drives, and the main cost after the war was providing pensions to the hundreds of thousands of elderly veterans. In some cases, pensions were paid out to surviving spouses into the 1950s. Civil War pensions made up 40% of the Federal budget during the 1890s.

■ RIGHT: A Confederate bill. The Southern economy suffered for years from the aftermath of the Civil War.

Chapter Eleven:

A Southern Perspective on

"the War for Southern Independence,"

by Southern Historian Paul Marcello

OUR HEROES
AND
OUR FLAGS

■ **ABOVE: Our heroes and our flag: a print showing full-length portraits of Robert E. Lee, Stonewall Jackson, and G.T. Beauregard, with four versions of the Confederate flag surrounded by bust portraits of Jefferson Davis and Confederate Army officers.**

In the popular culture and media accounts of the Civil War, Abraham Lincoln gained the Presidency and took the measures needed to end the institution of slavery. He led the country in a great war against the seceded slaveholding Southern states, brought them back in to the Union, and abolished slavery. As such, many Americans consider Abraham Lincoln as one of our greatest leaders. The people of the South have a different view of the war.

In schools both North and South, many American students are taught that it was wrong for anyone to take up arms in support of the Confederacy, or to perish for its ideals. In fact, such thinking has now reached the point where political groups wish to have the Confederate Battle Flag removed from all public areas, arguing that the flag is offensive to African-Americans because it commemorates slavery.

In the standard account, the Civil War was an outcome of our Founding Fathers' failure to address the institution of slavery in a republic that proclaimed in its Declaration of Independence that all men are created equal. But was it really necessary to wage a four-year war to abolish slavery in the United States? One that ravaged half of the

country and destroyed a generation of American men?

Southerners argue that the war did enable Lincoln to preserve the Union, but only in a geographic sense. The country had never really been a true union, nor was it conceived as one. It was conceived as a union of separate and sovereign states that evolved into a nation with a powerful, highly centralized Federal government. Therefore, though the war freed 4 million slaves, it also solidified a process of centralization that has substantially restricted liberty and freedom in America.

To Southerners, even the term "Civil War" is a misnomer, because the South did not instigate a rebellion. Thirteen Southern states in 1860 and 1861 simply chose to secede from the Union and go their own way as the 13 colonies did when they seceded from England in 1776. A more accurate name for the war that took place between the Northern and Southern American

ABOVE: Emancipated slaves traveling north with Lincoln's proclamation.

states is the War for Southern Independence. Unfortunately, the historians and the media present the victor's account—one that focuses on the issue of slavery and downplays other considerations.

In fact, slavery would have died out on its own. In 1807, the United States adopted a bill named the Act to Prohibit the Importation of Slaves. It prohibited bringing slaves into any port in the country, including into the Southern slaveholding states. Congress strengthened this prohibition in 1819 when it decreed the slave trade to be a form of piracy

and punishable by death. Article 1, Section 9 of The Constitution of the Confederate States of America prohibited the importation of slaves. With no fugitive slave laws in neighboring states that would return fugitive slaves to their owners, the value of slaves as property decreased due to inflated costs incurred to prevent their escape. When slaves had a place to escape to in the North, and with the supply of new slaves restricted by its Constitution, slavery in the Confederacy surely would have ended without a war. A slave's decreased property value would have made the institution quickly unsustainable.

If slavery were not the issue, then what was? For Northern business and political leaders, it was purely a financial matter. The largest source of tax revenue for the Federal government before the war was a tariff on imports. These tariffs were imposed by the Federal government not only to swell the

The first Flag of Independence raised

in the South, by the Citizens of Savannah, Ga. November 8th 1860.

Dedicated to the Morning News.

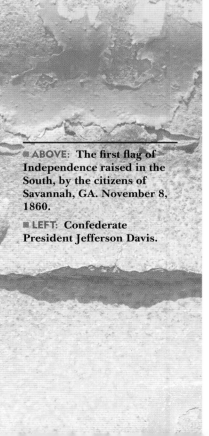

■ **ABOVE:** The first flag of Independence raised in the South, by the citizens of Savannah, GA. November 8, 1860.

■ **LEFT:** Confederate President Jefferson Davis.

Federal coffers, but also to raise the price of imported goods to a level where the less productive manufacturers of the northeast could be competitive. The North faced horrific financial problems if the Southern states became a separate republic on its border, one that engaged in free trade with England. If the Union was preserved, the South would lose millions. However, if the South seceded, the North would lose millions. In essence, the War Between the States was a tariff war; a war fought by the South for much the same reason that the American colonies fought the Revolutionary War. Recall that the American colony's chief grievance against England had

■ ABOVE: **The inauguration of Jefferson Davis as President, 1861.**

been English taxes. The South was therefore exasperated in March 1861 when Lincoln signed the Morrill Tariff into law—a tax much more draconian than the one forced on the American colonies in the 1770s.

Furthermore, slavery was not even the original Northern rallying cry at the beginning of the war. The war's stated aim was preservation of the Union and not the freeing of the slaves. Abolition was not the overriding public issue in 1861. Lincoln himself did not start the war as an abolitionist. In his 1861 inaugural address, he reassured slaveholders that his administration would continue to enforce the Fugitive Slave Act.

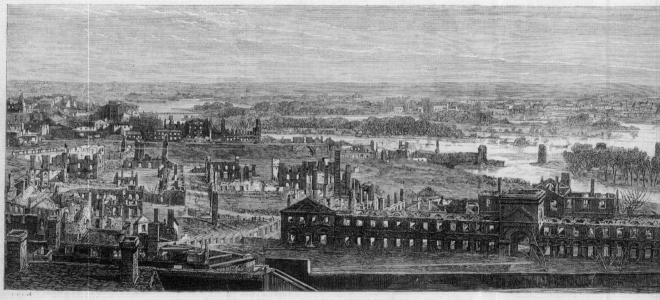

PANORAMA OF RICHMOND, VIRGINIA, AFTER ITS CAPTURE BY THE FEDERALS.—SEE NEXT PAGE.

When war came, Lincoln forced the Confederacy to fire the first shots of the war by dispatching ships with troops and arms to Fort Sumter, South Carolina. Charleston's militia was enraged, and bombarded the fort on April 12, 1861, resulting in its surrender. Union newspapers declared that the Southern secession was now an armed rebellion and called for Lincoln to put it down. Congress was adjourned and, for three months, Lincoln assumed dictatorial powers, raised an army, and

■ ABOVE: A panorama of the city of Richmond, Virginia (the top engraving joins with the lower one, end to end) in April 1865 when it was entered by Federal troops after the Confederacy had evacuated the city, its former capital. The Confederate Army accompanied its retreat by acts of incendiarism, causing the destruction of many offices, factories, shops, and houses.

shut down newspapers that disagreed with his war policies. He ordered the imprisonment of political opponents and suspended the Habeas Corpus and free speech rights of nonviolent dissenters. In an attempt to force the legally-seceded Southern states back into the Union, he called for 75,000 troops. At the time, only seven Southern states had seceded, but this inspired four more to do so. Again, Lincoln's aim was preservation of the Union, not slavery.

The first 17 months of the war

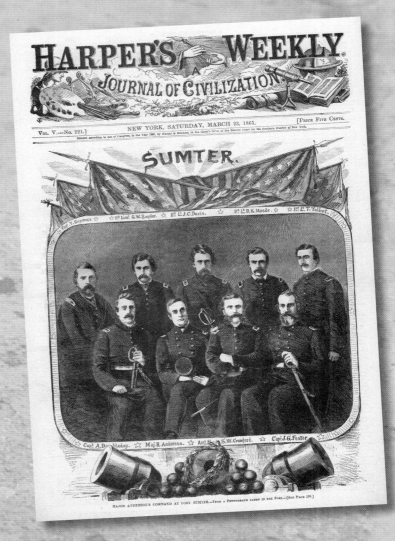

■ ABOVE: **American Civil War officers at Fort Sumter, as depicted by** *Harper's Weekly.*

did not go well for the Union Army, especially in the Eastern theater. The Union Army failed to win a decisive victory between July 1861 and September 1862. The Confederate Army of Northern Virginia won three decisive victories—at the battles of First Manassas, the Seven Days, and Sharpsburg. The Union leaders felt that a more visceral, emotional reason for continuing the fighting was needed than simple preservation of the Union. The war was dragging on. It had become apparent that the

Confederacy posed no threat to the Northern states and that perhaps the war wasn't worth the lives of thousands of young men.

On September 22, 1862, Abraham Lincoln issued his preliminary Emancipation Proclamation—both a new war measure and a brilliant piece of propaganda. Lincoln knew that he could not abolish slavery at the state level in the South. It would require a constitutional amendment.   Emancipation was also not universal. It would only affect those Confederate States not under Union control. Therefore, slaves in Missouri, Kentucky, Maryland, Delaware, Tennessee, and

the nation's capital were exempt.

During the war, the Constitution of the Confederate States of America forbade protectionist tariffs, outlawed government subsidies to private business, and made congressional appropriations subject to an approval by a two-thirds majority vote. It also forbade the Confederate Congress from initiating constitutional amendments, leaving that power to the states. It also limited its President to a single six-year term. It was, in many ways, a more enlightened document than the one in the North. However, when the Confederacy was defeated, it was defeated not by the original American republic of Thomas

Jefferson, committed to free trade and limited constitutional government, but a country that was now an empire ruled by a central authority. Lincoln had succeeded in his war aim, to preserve the Northern economy.

The War for Southern Independence caused deep racial and political wounds for Americans, both white and black, and the subsequent Reconstruction proved to be deep, brutal and long lasting. Freed slaves found that though Northern abolitionists wanted the slaves freed, they did not necessarily want them in their communities. In fact, Indiana and Illinois passed laws that barred African-Americans from residency.

At a gathering of Confederate veterans in 1870, General Robert E. Lee stated that "if I had foreseen the use those people had designed to make of their victory, there would have been no surrender at Appomattox Court House; no sir, not by me. Had I foreseen these results of subjugation, I would have preferred to die at Appomattox with my brave men, my sword in my right hand."

To Southerners, the failure of the Confederate States of America to win the War for Southern Independence was a blow to liberty, not only in the harsh 12-year military occupation and a Radical Republican Reconstruction, but also for basic principles of individual liberty and freedom. As we look back, let's hope that the Confederate Battle Flag will come to be viewed not as a symbol of slavery, which it certainly is not to Southerners, but as a symbol of opposition to central governmental power and tyranny.

■ **ABOVE: Honor the brave! An American Civil War memorial card.**

■ **RIGHT: The Confederate flag.**